D1568186

I Miss My Foster Parents

Stefon Herbert

Child Welfare League of America
Washington, DC

Child Welfare League of America, Inc.
440 First Street, NW, Suite 310, Washington, DC 20001-2085

CURRENT PRINTING (last digit)
10 9 8 7 6 5 4 3 2 1
Printed in the United States of America

ISBN # 0–87868–476–X

To Mom-mom and Pop-pop Mason,
with love.

When I was three years old my sister and I went to live with foster parents.

We called them
Mom-mom and Pop-pop.

Sometimes other children
came to live in the house.

I liked to help Pop-pop
take things off his truck.

Sometimes I sat on Pop-pop's
lap to watch football
on t.v.

I liked to watch Billy
play catch.

One day Mom-mom told me and my sister that a family wanted to adopt us.

I felt sad.
My sister was scared.

We didn't want to leave Mom-mom and Pop-pop. We didn't want to leave our friends.

First we had overnight visits with our new family.

I did not like the overnight visits. My new family lived in the country. They had a cat and the mosquitoes kept biting me.

Then Mom-mom packed our clothes and we moved to live with our adoptive family.

Now I'm used to my new home and new friends. Shelly is a nice cat.

But I still miss
Mom-mom and Pop-pop.

I feel real happy when I talk to them on the telephone or send them cards.

Maybe some day my sister and I can spend the night with Mom-mom and Pop-pop.